WILLED

IGNORANCE

THE UNSPOKEN PANDEMIC

Cover & Interior Formatting by Platform House
www.platformhouseublishing.com

For my children.
For you, your spouse, children, relatives, or friends.

For ALL the ones we love.

For those of you that know me, you know that I write like I talk. I can't say that this will be grammatically correct. The past and present tense could be used in the same sentence. I live in the present. I'm talking about the past.

This is a heartbreaking story about suicide.
This story is about loss, but also can be about hope-
IF we start having a conversation now.

I initially wrote this in 1999 as a way for me to process and remember. I've made additional inserts, updates, comments, and thoughts, as I've had two decades to reflect on the impact.

This was also written for my children and strangers, in hopes that one day you will know and learn from my experiences.

It's now the year 2023 and the world is still in chaos over the COVID-19 pandemic. A pandemic is defined as a disease that is prevalent over a whole country or world. A list of a few that you might have heard of in last century:

Name	Date	Global Deaths
COVID-19	2020-Present	6.7 million *
HIV/Aids	1981-Present	36 million *
Flu Pandemic	1968	1 million
Asian Flu	1956-1958	2 million
Sixth Cholera	1910-1911	800,000

The one pandemic you probably have not heard about or read of is SUICIDE.

There are over 800,000 worldwide deaths by suicide PER YEAR.

And the number is GROWING...

The United States suicide rate was reported with a thirty percent increase since 1999. As of 2018, all states increased in suicides rates, with the exception of Nevada. [1]

Firearms are the most common choice of method.

In 1999, there were 29,199 suicides in the United States. [2]

In 2017, there was 47,173. It is the second leading cause of death in ages 15 to 34, and third for ages 10 to 14. [3]

Among U.S. adults, the average number of suicides per day rose from 86.6 in 2005 to 124.4 in 2017. These numbers included 15.9 veteran suicides per day in 2005 and 16.8 in 2017.

In 2017, the suicide rate for veterans was 1.5 times the rate for non-veteran adults, after adjusting for population differences in age and sex. [4]

It's time we had a serious talk.

1. NBC news, 6/7/2018 by Maggie Fox
https://www.nbcnews.com/health/health-news/suicide-rates-are-30-percent-1999-cdc-says-n880926
2. CDC 12/14/2007 Morbidity and Mortality Weekly Report
https://www.cdc.gov/mmwr/preview/mmwrhtml/mm5649a1.htm
3. Wikipedia, Suicide in the US and American Foundation for Suicide Prevention, Suicide Facts and Figures United States 2019.
4. Mental Health.VA.Gov 2019 National Veterans Suicide Prevention Annual Report

Forward

Vain

(van). adj.
{ ME. < Ofr. < L. Vanus, empty, vain, for IE base see WANT}
1. *having no real value or significance; worthless, empty, idle.*
2. *without force or effect, futile, fruitless, unprofitable, unavailing.*
3. *having of showing an excessively high regard for one's self, looks, possessions, ability. Indulging in or resulting from personal vanity, conceit.*

They all agree that the first sign after a suicide is NUMBNESS. Not for me. The first thing I thought of was VANITY. Have you ever seen the movie The Devil's Advocate? It features Al Pacino and Keanu Reeves. My husband and I have seen it dozens of times. What I kept thinking of was the last line where Al Pacino, who portrays Satan, says, in essence, how vanity was his favorite sin because it would lead you to fail each time.

So, I guess that's how I felt. A failure. Vanity = failure. I think I'll write Webster and tell them to add this as #4 for definitions. I always thought that vanity was #3, above. Thus, if one were vain, one would not kill thyself. Especially not in a gruesome manner. Don't want to mess up that pretty face, now, do we? And SUICIDE? This couldn't happen to me. I'm college educated. I have a BS with two degrees. I'm a vice president and equity partner in a private company. Young. Living. A wife. A mother to two. A friend.

To my list of titles, I can now add, SOS…Survivor of Suicide.

My husband is the most intelligent person I know. No formal education, but book smart and street smart. A real savvy person. Handsome, too. Tall, 6'1, brown hair and eyes, lean, and a great dresser. Personable…God, is he personable. Can make everyone he meets smile; everyone knows him. He can make me laugh, even when I'm mad at him. He's charming. Young. Husband. A father. My husband even owns his own businesses. Two.

We have a charmed and blessed life. Two beautiful newborn twins, a boy and a girl! A big, beautiful, white house. A dog, a cat, and 15 fish. What more can you ask for?

We have one more title we can add to our list. WIDOW.

My husband is now dead.

My children and I are the survivors.

"Suicide rates from firearms are particularly high in the US – 60% of deaths are from firearms result from suicide."
-Suicide by Hannah Ritchie, Max Rosner and Esteban Ortiz-Ospina.

Let's change this statistic.
Reach out to the ones you love.

JANUARY 1998

Journey

Life's adventures. You never know where they'll take you or when they will begin. My husband, Charlie, and I had known each other for 10 years before we started dating. I knew him through his marriage (and subsequent divorce) and through his girlfriends, past and present. He, too, knew me through a myriad of bad choices, good times, and friendship. For many years he was my best friend. We spent every day together. Then, through the years we would touch base, but our lives had gone in different directions with him being married and me being on the single scene. Dallas is a big city, and the likelihood of seeing someone out is like winning the lottery. Slim to none, but you keep trying.

Roughly ten years later, I had no idea that on that cold January day when I met Charlie for happy hour, my life would be changed...forever. After he separated from his wife, he would call me to meet. I blew him off several times. I remember thinking, "No time, bud. I don't want to hear any more depressing stories. I have enough of my own." Knowing Charlie through many non-sober nights, I figured he just wanted to drink and be merry. After all, that was our favorite

1

(and mainly only) pastime. Finally, after enough badgering, I met him at my favorite local restaurant/bar. They serve many cold drinks and adequate food, and everyone knows each other. Similar to "Cheers", but with a Cajun twist and a little bit racier crowd.

I knew when he walked in the door that we would be together. He knew, too, long before.

We talked, we drank, and we danced. Time had stopped for us. If you ever wonder what it feels like to be on a pedestal, I can tell you. I felt like Peter Pan. Flying—no, soaring—through the air. Or, maybe it's like being a rock star and having thousands of people cheer you on, or maybe yet, skydiving into a sea of clouds that all want to hold and comfort you. All wanting to be like you, with you. You are suddenly slimmer, prettier, and more elegant than mere moments before. Charlie adored me. He held me high on this pedestal, worshiping me. I was a goddess, and he was my savior.

Other people know when they see people in love. They are envious, jealous, and even angry. Angry that they can't remember, angry that they let themselves lose that feeling. I saw that look when people saw Charlie and I together.

And to think…just yesterday, I was one of them.

Charlie asked me to marry him that same night. I thought to myself, just as I did 5 years ago when he'd asked before, *"We already are."*

When you start that journey down an unknowing road…what are the feelings that you go through? Are you nervous? Anxious? Hesitant? Can you think? Can you remember?

I remember. I remember what I felt. It was pure *Bliss.*

What I didn't remember, and what common sense should have reminded me, is that a pedestal will fall.

What is one of the leading causes of deaths for young people? Suicide.

Let's change this statistic.

FEBRUARY 1998

Hardship

Roughly one month after we started dating, I left Charlie's side for the first time to take care of my sister's children while she and her husband went on vacation for a week. She lived in Nebraska, of all places.

Charlie has always been co-dependent. That's probably why he got married in the first place (the first time). He couldn't stand to be alone. Ever. He bought a dog a couple of years back. He said it was for hunting, but I really think it was so he would never have to be by himself. He drove with that big dog in his jeep. He took it to work and slept with it, too. The dog was afraid of guns and birds. Loveable ol' mutt.

I was in Nebraska for only three days when I got the call. It had occurred eight hours before I even found out. Charlie was driving through an intersection near his house when an 18-wheeler didn't stop for a red light. The eighteen-wheeler was carrying who knows how many tons of rocks and cement. Charlie was driving his beloved Jeep Sahara. With a lift kit on it, of course. It's a good thing. As the truck drove at 70 mph, it hit him directly at the driver's side door of Charlie's jeep. They say the roll bar was the only thing that stopped the truck from hitting his head directly. Some still say that it was Charlie's head that stopped the truck.

He was unconscious. Punctured lung, broken ribs, slivered spleen and liver, severe laceration of the head. Those were the physical problems.

They had to care flight him to a downtown hospital. With three kids in tow, I yanked them out of school, packed, and flew back, but couldn't get there until the next day. I still remember what Charlie said when he saw me... *"Hey there, gorgeous. How are you doing, baby?"* My pain stopped. The fear subsided. I figured he must be OK. He was tough. Young. He had already been through a motorcycle accident and neck surgery. He would make it through this. To be with me, at least. The nieces and nephews had a field day with my friends while I tended to Charlie in the hospital. His family arrived and so did some unwelcomed others. Ah, the old saying goes: when you marry a person, you get with them their family, friends, and past. My family is as dysfunctional as the rest, but they're my family. You know how it is.

For 5 days we camped out at the hospital, each day resurrecting for Charlie the previous day's activities. Although Charlie was progressing physically, he had no recollection from the accident or during his stay at the hospital. It was like the movie *"Groundhog Day."* The doctors assured us that this was temporary and would pass. In some respects, it never did.

For the several weeks, we attended a slew of physical and mental therapy. My work graciously allowed me to work from home. (Charlie and I had lived together since that first night.) It had been so long since anyone at work had actually seen me with a man, not to mention happy, I think they wanted to do anything to help assure that I would stay that way.

At times, Charlie appeared very coherent, talking to friends, business partners, etc. It wasn't until the next day that you realized he had no knowledge of what had happened the day before. It was very misleading, at times. He looked good and sounded good, but there was something not quite right.

The progression from therapy was very slow. Charlie still had no recollection since the accident occurred. The medication he was on would wipe him out or make him wired. The physical therapy was strenuous and a painful reminder of what he had been through not even a year ago with major neck surgery on his 5th and 6th vertebrae. I was exhausted from taking care of him, dealing with outside family and visitors, working from home, and trying to sort out just what was ahead of us. Not to mention the lawsuits that would be pending against the trucker. I was constantly reminded by Charlie's lawyers to keep track of what he was doing and keep him out of trouble. That's like keeping a kid away from an open candy jar.

All the while, my father was at home taking care of my mother, who suffered from a stroke that had occurred 20 years ago. I envisioned that this was what was looming ahead for us.

I wasn't even married.

Suddenly, I felt *tired*.

The distress signal "SOS" stands for more than 'Save Our Ship' but was also originally considered for 'Save Our Souls.'

It also stands for 'Survivor of Suicide.'

Let's focus on "Survivor".

MARCH 1998

Denial

By mid-March, Charlie and I decided to have him stop the neurological prescribed medication. Within one day, he was back to normal, calling customers and friends and remembering the next day, too. Maybe he remembered too much.

Within two days after being off medication, he explained to me that he needed his space. After all, he didn't want to jump into another situation. He was scared. Plain and simple. I don't blame him. He didn't have control over the truck that hit him, and I can't say as I'm one to be controlled. This man had to rely on me, and it was scary. The loss of independence is a terrible thing after you've attained it.

What really tormented Charlie was that he'd lived. He started drinking heavily to forget. Night after night, as he became more and more incoherent, he asked himself - *why?why?why?*

Charlie didn't believe in himself. In his mind, for the wrongs that he had committed in his life, he felt that his life should have been taken with that truck. His sins are no worse or better than the next person. Mine either, for that matter. But Charlie did grow up with this deep belief. He was Mormon, I was Catholic. He was much more versed and fluent in religion than I'll ever be. We used to debate all the time and call our dads to settle our disputes. We debated about everything. It was a sportsman like competition. It was power—no, more like foreplay.

In my experience, most people who survive a devastating event turn to religion. Charlie turned away from it. He was angry that he lived. He couldn't understand and rationalize. In his mind, he deserved to die. He wanted to die. He wanted to complete the self-fulfilling prophecy.

In the ten previous years that I knew Charlie before we started dating, he had threatened suicide on more than one occasion. It always occurred under the influence of excessive alcohol. I just thought it was because he was real immature. Not to mention, he couldn't hold his liquor.

Never considering suicide myself, it was hard to relate to someone who did. You may think of the stigma of suicide as weakness. For me, I thought additionally: lower class, immaturity, alcoholism, and attention deficit disorder. Why else would you commit but not follow through? As if you were raising your hand to say, *"Hey, I need some attention, here. Look at me. I want to be the center of your universe. Me, me, me."* I used to call it the Cyclops Syndrome…just focusing on the one "I". I don't think this way anymore. Suicidal people don't want to die, they just want the pain to stop.

March was a hard month. You know that feeling you get when you stop seeing someone? The pit in your stomach that aches physically and mentally? You can't sleep, you can't think, constantly playing over in your mind the 'what ifs' or 'if I changed this.' Nothing but time changes it.

Charlie and I hadn't gone out that long, but we'd known each other for over 10 years, being the best of friends for many of those years. I'd had only several other long-term relationships, the ones that you actually can count that lasted more than the one night. I knew this was supposed to be. I knew everything about Charlie, and he knew about me. I accepted him knowing all this.

I traveled a lot for my work and was reading a John Grisham book during one of my trips. Can't recall which novel, but I remember I tore out the last pages to give to Charlie. It explained how he was and how he felt. He cried. Someone understood how he felt. He was no longer alone.

He told me he came back to me because he realized the significance in that I'd packed up three kids from Nebraska and came back to be with him. (He jokingly said it was because I was the only girl that he knew who could buy her own SUV outright.) He felt that no one else would have come back for him. That was partially true. I came back because I knew he was part of my future.

In a matter of one month, I had been on a roller coaster ride of emotions. Charlie, too. But now we knew that we were meant for each other, forever. Starting off the month with denial led us to our future.

I do believe there are "signs" everywhere…if you read them.

**Know the warning signs of suicide and call
a crisis line: 1-800-SUICIDE or 988**

- Talking about wanting to die or killing oneself
- Increased use of drugs/alcohol
- Anxiousness
- Sleeping too little or too much
- Mood swings
- Talking about feeling hopeless or no purpose.
- Being withdrawn or isolated

**We need each other.
We need more in-depth conversations
and less judgment.**

APRIL 1998

Joy. Happy. Happy. Joy. Joy.

Nothing like being in love in April. Or any other month, for that matter. But in Dallas, April is a great month. Not too hot, not too cool, before May showers, and a lot of patios to sit and drink on. I think Charlie and I hit every one of them. We met friends, drank merrily, laughed, kissed, and more.

And then did it again the next day.

Although we had been living together since January (except for his two-week escapade in March), Charlie wanted us to get married and LIVE together. Remember: co-dependent. After just feeling recently burned, I was a little hesitant, to say the least. We had decided that if all went smoothly, we could get married in the September-October time frame and then would try to start having children in December. Both of us wanted children, for much different reasons. I think Charlie wanted them to give him hope, and me—well, to give me my purpose. We talked about how it would change our carefree lives and agreed that it was what we both wanted. And needed. And the next day on the patio, we talked about it again…

April was a bonus month for me, too. As an equity partner

in a top 10 cable firm, we were bought out by "Mr. Wired World" himself, Paul Allen. We all received a nice chuck of change and were guaranteed that we would retain management responsibilities. How cool was that? Got bought out and continued to get paid for doing the same thing. Cable TV was my friend.

After hearing that most of my friends had been having trouble becoming pregnant, Charlie wanted me to get off the pill. He teased that I wasn't getting any younger and reminded me that I was four years older than he was. I didn't have any objections to it. After all, I really didn't think I could get pregnant. Goes back to being raised Catholic. I figured that for all my sins (many), I wouldn't be rewarded with being able to carry another human life.

Charlie was always so doting on me. He'd bring me flowers for no occasion. Tell me a thousand times a day just how gorgeous I was or how much he loved me. He was just that way. He literally would give the shirt off his back to a stranger and would do even more for a friend. Very generous. Too much so, at times. In some ways, I felt that he was trying to buy friendship or loyalty. I recognized this, as I used to do the same. Some of his family or friends took advantage of Charlie many times. He was always there if they needed him. They never had to learn to be self-reliant—they had Charlie.

Each day was a new beginning for us. We looked forward to our future together and started planning our lives. I got off the pill.

It didn't take us as long as it did for my friends to get pregnant…

"...suicidal thoughts and behaviors start when vulnerable individuals encounter stressful events, become overwhelmed, and conclude that suicide is the only reasonable way (given their very likely biased way of thinking) to stop the pain they are experiencing. Determining what makes events stressful is difficult because of the highly individual nature of human coping abilities and perspectives. What may seem relatively trivial to one person may seem devastating or insurmountable to another."
— MentalHealth.net

Life can be hard.
Be kind.

MAY 1998

Beginnings

Yep, it didn't take us quite as long to get pregnant as we thought. In fact, it took 2 weeks. When I told him that we needed to get a pregnancy test after he picked me up from work, he called 30 more times than usual to just check and see how I was doing at the office.

We stopped off at a local drugstore then visited a sandwich shop, on the way home. I was never late for a period, but figured it was just nerves and from getting off the pill after 15 years. Charlie started on his sandwich, and I went to the bathroom. Minutes later, I came into the living room to show him the results. We thought there was a blue line but couldn't be sure. My nerves were now racing. I wanted him to go back to the store to get another type of test. He asked if he could finish his sandwich. I gave him *THE* look. He left immediately and returned just as fast. I think that during the drive to the store, it hit him that we were, indeed, pregnant. My stomach soared and yet sank. I'm sure his did, too. He returned and immediately went to the bathroom. I redid the test, and it was positive. No doubt. + equals pregnant. Charlie didn't come out for what seemed like an eternity. As he came out, he smiled and simply said, "Are we happy?" I cried.

Life just changed. For the better.

That evening, we drove to the horse races for a cable event. On the drive, Charlie kept repeatedly saying, "Wow...wow...WOW." I didn't say a word. It was all too surreal. We didn't stay at the races long. I knew my colleagues would wonder if they saw me drinking soda water all night. We exchanged glances across the room during unremembered conversations with others, giving each other that look of knowing something that no one else did. I had a sense of peace, contentment, and confirmation.

We excitedly drove home and laid in bed talking about our soon-to-be new life. I told him we needed to be careful who we told, at least for 12 weeks. I fell asleep exhausted, still able to hear Charlie on the phone telling everyone he knew our good news.

Charlie was always so attentive, making sure I ate right, massaged my feet, and told friends not to call so I could get my sleep. He was in seventh heaven.

It was not even a week later, when I was away on a business/vacation trip in Aruba, that the doctors told Charlie that there may be a chance he had an aneurysm, based on an MRI. They couldn't be sure until the specialist reviewed the film, and he wouldn't be back until the following week. Once again, I was confronted with horrendous news while I was away. This time, I didn't return home. There was nothing that I could do, and I felt that the doctors were pre-warning him of the worst scenario versus the actuality. I couldn't imagine that we both would be given the chance to give life and then have this occur. My faith and hope told me this couldn't be so.

Looking back, I think this was the precipitating event that started the pathway to Charlie completing suicide. The fact I didn't come back resurrected his depression.

When I returned, the doctor phoned and said they agreed that they thought this could be treated with medication versus surgery. What a relief. Charlie went through more tests and more debilitating medication. The medication made him loopy, as if he was drugged or whacked out. He couldn't stand to be out of control or not in control. He stopped taking the medication. The symptoms of physical pain now suddenly started to appear.

On his birthday at the end of the month, we went out to celebrate with him drinking heavily and me as the designated driver. By the end of the evening, he was in a fiery fit, and told me that he wasn't going to go through "this" again. He had already been married unhappily once. He'd pay child support and could be a good father. I couldn't believe I was hearing this. I was thinking, *"Are you f---ing crazy?"* As I started to leave, he stopped me, concerned that I was too hysterical to be driving in my condition. In *MY* condition?!

We went inside and calmed down just as his mother called to wish him happy birthday. He glowed as he talked about recent and past events, and all the while I steamed. He told me everything would be ok. It wasn't.

Over and over, I thought...this is just the Beginning.

Both negative and positive events can be sources of significant stress. Examples of events that cause positive stress include marriage, moving (when it is a desired move), having a child, and changing jobs (when that is desired).
https://www.mentalhelp.net

Stress is STRESS.
Let's help each other out!

JUNE 1998

Commitment

Charlie had the ring in his pocket for a whole day. He couldn't stand it anymore. He called to meet. I told him let's just go to a local TGIF, since it was in-between our offices. I arrived early and ordered "pot stickers" for an appetizer. He arrived with one of his employees and asked excitedly if I wanted to see what was in his pocket. Figuring this was some sexual joke, I told him to lay it out. Behold—he placed a ring box on the table. I looked at him questioningly. Just days before, he'd asked what kind of ring I wanted. I told him anything as long as it wasn't round. Here before me on the table lay the largest, round diamond solitaire I had ever seen. I simply smiled and said, *"Big round is nice."* No formal asking, cordials, or anything else. He smiled with his chest puffed up and proud and me still in shock. We ate lunch and left to go back to work. I called everyone on my mobile.

The next day, I laughed as the glare from my ring made the car driver next to me stop and stare. Big round was pretty.

After 10+ years, I thought it best that he meet my parents. I wouldn't wear the ring, and this made Charlie somewhat disappointed, but I felt I couldn't go there and say, *"Hey, here he is, and by the way, we're pregnant, getting married, and looking for a new house."* My parents are cool, but at 65, I thought this might be pushing it.

My mom loved him at first sight. What wasn't there to love? Dad was a dad; they always have reservations, especially when it's your last baby girl.

We then journeyed to Alaska for a little quality time with his dad (and more importantly, fishing). Ah, what beautiful surroundings to celebrate our commitment. It was perfect, even though we were with his dad in a one-room cabin. So much for spontaneity. Charlie cringed when I caught the first fish (I also caught the biggest). We laughed and giggled and just enjoyed.

At night, Charlie used to wake me up with his sleep talking and walking. I was extremely exhausted during the first trimester and Charlie was notorious for waking me up at 2am to kiss my belly and tell me how much he loved me. It drove me wild, but how can you really complain about that? I mean, I can think of worse things. Then he'd wake up around 4am to make a peanut butter and jelly sandwich and then wake me up again to tell me some joke or something he'd thought of. We'd laugh until we cried. Ever since Charlie was a kid, he had been getting up at night to make himself a PB&J sandwich. *It's amazing the things you will miss.*

We had a sonogram done early. Based on my mother's and sister medical history, I figured it would be better to do it early. As the doctor probed over my stomach, she asked Charlie if he noticed anything wrong. I already knew. As Charlie hesitated, he then noticed that there was more than one. We were not only pregnant, but also blessed with twins. Charlie wept. He was so happy. I'm sure he thought he no longer needed the dog. Now he always had a reason to drive in the HOV lane. We laughed until we cried, thinking of all the new beginnings. TWO educations, TWO cars, TWO weddings…Ah, what if they were TWO girls? We laughed even harder.

I radiated. I loved being pregnant. I never felt better physically or mentally. It wasn't just the pregnancy. It was the start of a new life (or in our case, new lives). I just knew that this was a sign from above that all would finally go smoothly.

"The most frequent stressful event leading up to suicide (what is often called a precipitating event) in the US today is mental illness, which is estimated to account for about 90 percent of all suicides. As we discussed earlier, a newly diagnosed and/or poorly treated mental illness can trigger a suicide in some cases."
https://www.mentalhelp.net

Doctor visits are now even available online.
Seek professional help.

July 1998

Foundation

Ok, we were pregnant with twins, engaged, planning marriage, with his dog and my cat...now we needed a new place of our own together. Charlie had sold his other house and we started our search for a new place. We found it in less than a week in typical Charlie fashion.

As he was working on one of his client's computers, the highly intoxicated, newly divorced client of Charlie's stated that he wanted to get rid of his house and any remnants of his previous wife. Not one to let an opportunity go by, Charlie took him out for a little fun, sun, and more drinks to negotiate the price. Several hours later and after a large bar tab, he got the house for probably $20,000 under market value. That was good, since it was still $50,000 more than we wanted to pay.

I called my dad and asked him if the stock market was closed, and also asked if he was working on my account. After all, I was about to tell him big news. I couldn't afford for him to make a mistake on my account. I started by telling him that he was going to be a grandfather again. *"Oh, really"* was how he started his reply. Then, I told him that he was going to be a grandfather to twins, his youngest child was buying a house, and that she was also going to get married. He didn't pass out, so I took that as a good sign. Mom asked who was pregnant, then asked who the father was. She was glad to hear it was Charlie. She really liked him.

By the end of the month, we had the house deal done and moved in. When Charlie saw something he wanted, he bought it. He was never known to exercise a lot of patience. This was one of his best and worse traits.

With twin sets of furniture, one dog, and one fat cat, we moved in. It was liberating...it was freedom. No past memories, only future ones to make.

We sat on the back porch overlooking the pool with the old-timey streetlight and smiled. We skinny-dipped in *OUR* pool of *OUR* house with *OUR* unborn children. We talked about *OUR* plans, *OUR* future, and *OUR* lives.

A letter can change and make a whole new word. Who would have guessed that one day *"our"* would end up being *"Your"*?

Men die of suicide 3.5x more often than women.
Women are 1.4x more likely to attempt suicide.
https://afsp.org/suicide-statistics

Let's change these statistics.

AUGUST 1998

Ceremonious

T he thought of having the children out of wedlock drove Charlie crazy. Being raised by his adoptive stepfather, family meant everything to Charlie. He never took his family for granted. He cherished them. You don't see this type of loyalty anymore, especially if you knew some of the situations that his family and extended family had. I think I'm family oriented, but with Charlie, it was almost patriotic with his loyalty.

After being in the house for one week, Charlie decided that we needed to get married, and that Friday of the upcoming week was a good day.

On August 7, 1998, at 4:00pm at the Plano Justice of the Peace, in front of his brother and one of my best friends, we exchanged vows. The whole ceremony lasted 5 minutes. It would have been shorter, but I was crying so much, the Justice stopped to get a box of Kleenex. Charlie was dressed in a pair of khakis and a collarless shirt and I in a brown frumpy maternity dress. After we decided that we were going to get married, neither of us had much conversation about it nor made a big deal of it to each other. We already felt married. Always had.

I didn't think I would cry. I always felt that I'd never have a big ceremony. I had cried the entire night before, but for other reasons. I didn't have a wedding band, I couldn't fit into any outfits, I felt bloated, one of my friends couldn't show up...you name it. I blamed it on hormones. Charlie brought me 12 dozen handpicked roses in a big, beautiful wicker basket for our wedding day. They were breathtaking. He also got me a flower arrangement for the Justice of the Peace. He was always incredibly considerate and sensitive about those types of things. I got him a card. Woowee.

After the ceremony, we had a few friends to the house to celebrate the big event. Close friends of mine made us a videotape of the night's happenings. The tape had on it Grandma playing the harmonica and friends toasting and roasting us. I made a very humorous toast stating I wanted to live in peace and harmony. Charlie's toast was much more sentimental and enduring. I'll never forget it. Charlie turned to me and said, in less than 10 words, what any spouse would wait a lifetime to hear "To my wife, my children, my life."

He believed that 'til the day he died. I had no idea that the next ceremony I would have to attend, I would have to do ALONE. It would be for Charlie.

"Ninety percent of those who died by suicide had a diagnosable mental health condition at the time of their death."
https://afsp.org/suicide-statistics

Doctor visits are now even available online.
Seek professional help.
Get a second opinion if possible.

SEPTEMBER 1998

Introduction

Given both our sordid pasts, Charlie and I had an understanding. If you ever didn't make it home at night, don't bother coming back. It wasn't even a month after our wedding that Charlie called and said he'd be home at midnight. At 2am, I still hadn't heard from him.

Being 5 months pregnant, I hadn't wanted to go to a party that night but wanted Charlie to be able to get out. As I sat waiting for him, pacing the house, I had a premonition that this was going to be another start of something awful. I cried and cried. Then I decided to watch our fish, to calm me down. Over the month, we had purchased about $200 worth of fish and had successfully killed each one off. I was hoping that this time it would be different. It wasn't. As I sat and watched the one pregnant fish gasping for life, I felt the same. Drowning. I watched helplessly as the fish struggled to survive. At 5am, it gave up and floated to the top. I had been watching it for hours. My body cringed and I felt that my soul had lost something.

It was then that I felt the kids kick for the first time. At first, I thought I had just imagined it. Then it happened again. The euphoria was lost knowing that my husband wasn't home to share it with me. Another first missed.

Charlie called at 4am to say he wasn't coming home. He knew what this meant. The battleground had been drawn. If I allowed him to come back, I compromised my standards and credibility. I kept thinking, *"Why? I'm five months pregnant with twins and just got married!"* I didn't sleep all night.

Charlie came home at noon the next day. The demons were loose. He had pure hatred for me. I couldn't understand why. He told me that he wanted a DNA test done on the children. Right then, I knew. It wasn't me; it was him. Guilt will make you do and say terrible things. This wasn't Charlie talking.

He slept 'til the evening. When he awoke, he saw me crying in the bedroom and apologized. Said it wouldn't happen again. I cried more, for I knew it had just started. I kept thinking; *I am five months pregnant. The twins just kicked for the first time, and you weren't here to share in it.* My defenses were coming up. I didn't want that to happen, for I knew what it meant. I'd do it alone.

Two weeks later, Charlie didn't come home AGAIN.

"In addition to major depression, depressive symptoms may also be caused by bipolar disorder, or may co-occur with another disorder. Bipolar disorder is typically characterized by alternations of mood and energy levels occurring over months, weeks or days. Symptoms may include periods of hyperactivity, fast speech, expansive sexuality, lack of need for sleep and feelings of inflated-well being; and corresponding periods of depression where some or all of the symptoms listed above are present."
https://www.mentalhelp.net

Be alert and know the signs!

OCTOBER 1998

Miracles

T hings started to settle down on the home front at the beginning of the month. I don't know why; it must have been the calm before the storm.

Since we didn't have a formal wedding, but a visit to the JOP, we had our reception in October. Friends and family gathered around to celebrate our nuptials and children. It was a good thing we had the reception early in the month, because we didn't know that we would be delivering just two weeks later.

Sunday, October 25th started out like any other Sunday. We slept in, piddled in the yard, and killed more fish in our tank while Charlie simmered a pot roast. My back had been aching all day. I figured it was just from the 22 extra pounds I was carrying on my 5'4" frame. After dinner, I lay in discomfort, trying to pay attention to the ball game. Charlie had pampered me all day. He was very giving in that way. He cooked for me, rubbed my shoulders, feet, etc. He made me baths and washed my hair. He would have done this regardless of if I was pregnant.

By nightfall, I was doubled over in pain. We called a friend who'd recently delivered with our same doctor, then we called our doctor. She told us to get the hospital immediately. We lived one mile away. What a sight I must have looked. I had just taken a bath and didn't even brush my hair. Charlie was so nervous, he dressed me in a sack. He ran two lights getting to the hospital.

I was sure it was just cramps, or even worse, indigestion from the spicy pot roast. Charlie always over-seasoned everything. It wasn't. My water had broken. I was over 4 centimeters dilated and our son's hand was sticking out. It was time to deliver. Within 45 minutes, I had been prepped and was on the table. Charlie was there with me every second.

At 12:05 and 12:07am, just under 2 hours from when we arrived, our son and our daughter joined us in this world. Weighing just 2.4 and 2.1 pounds, respectively, they were immediately rushed to NICU. I never had any fear for them or for me during the delivery. Charlie, on the other hand, had more than his share of fear for all of us.

It wasn't 'til days later that he would tell me during my emergency c-section, he saw them take my insides and place them on my stomach to deliver our children. The whole time, he wondered if he was going to lose all three of us at once. Wondering if they make coffins for babies, and do you put them in separate ones, or should he put all of us together? It must have been hell for him.

Whatever I needed in the hospital, Charlie was there to get it, do it, or find it. He took friends and relatives to the NICU ward at all hours of the day and night to show off the kids. He couldn't wait 'til the next person came so he could show them off again.

The kids made great progress, in comparison to many of the other children in the ward. They had tubes sticking out of their hands or foreheads, IVs, things to help them breathe, oxygen tents, and so much more. To us, they were precious little miracles.

Two days after we arrived, our doctor came to see me. Charlie had just left to get some things at the house. What she told me threw me and would throw us for another loop. My blood test had come back with positive results. Positive for HIV. I sat there in bewilderment. How could this be? She told me she thought this was a false positive test, but felt she needed to tell me until we could take another test to confirm. I knew there was no way it was from me. Ever since I got hepatitis, I'd had my blood checked every 6 months. I hadn't been with another man in over 2 years. I was just tested in May. It wasn't me. The things that ran through my mind were: Where did Charlie sleep those nights away? And with whom?

I called Charlie and told him to come back immediately. I was crying so hard that I couldn't get it out for almost a half hour. He sat there dumbfounded, too. Then we cried together. The only thing he said was, *"We'll get through this."*

It took 9 (that would be NINE) days for the tests to come back. They came back negative, just as the doctor had suspected. The harm that it did was irreparable, in a sense. Just as I'd had doubts, so did Charlie. The questioning about DNA and paternity came back – over and over. The thought of these children not being his killed Charlie's will. This is how he rationalized being alive.

As Charlie anguished mentally, his physical pain from the accident also returned. He started having numbness and sharp pains down his neck and arm. It scared him.

Somehow, we would get over this, too. Time can heal everything. I just didn't realize that time was running out.

"Determining what makes events stressful is difficult because of the highly individual nature of human coping abilities and perspectives. What may seem relatively trivial to one person may seem devastating or insurmountable to another."
https://www.mentalhelp.net/articles/suicide/

Be a no judgement zone for others.

NOVEMBER 1998

Momentum

At first, as I was trying to write this and think back, I couldn't recall what occurred this month, and was relieved momentarily, thinking that nothing had happened. It took only a couple of seconds to change my mind.

Days passed in the NICU, we watched the triumphs and falls of our children. I would go there each morning and "kangaroo" with the kids. This is where you place them on your bare chest so they can feel your warmth and hear your heartbeat. It's supposed to be relaxing for them. For me, it wasn't. I would have to kangaroo with each child for 3 hours at a time while taking a break to breast pump and then start again for another 3 hours with the next child. Charlie and I together would then return each night to do it again. It was exhausting.

Charlie was actively trying to expand his business. He knew that the likelihood of me wanting to go back to work or being able to go back to work was slim because of the kids' condition. He decided that he needed to do something else, so we could live off one income. It was very stressful for him. On top of everything else.

Both of us could spend money like it was water. Neither of us tended to look at price tags, Charlie more so than I. He had extravagant tastes and certainly could pick out better clothes for me than I could myself. I have practical taste. Knowing how we spent money, it worried Charlie how we would make out on one income. I was fortunate enough to have money due to my company. Charlie didn't want to have to survive on his wife's income. Most men wouldn't. And, I can't say I wanted to wear the "pants" in the family. Remember: practical.

Charlie's physical pain was increasing. The medication that he stopped taking earlier in the year was for stimulating the brain activity and stated that without medication, stress could enhance the effects and cause depression, stimulus, etc. No one ever reads the fine print and, in my opinion, doctors these days certainly don't explain the severity enough.

To add to this, my c-section was infected, and I also had a breast infection from pumping and was scheduling doctors in between kangarooing with the kids.

Reluctantly, Charlie returned to his original neck doctor to get a checkup. He had to have more MRIs and other x-rays. How he hated this. Three days before he was scheduled to go on his first real hunt in over a year, the doctor informed us that Charlie had another problem with his vertebrae in his neck. He already had two fused together 18 months ago, and now he would have to have the two under those fused, also. This would literally cause a block in his neck, limiting how he would live for the rest of his life. The doctor told him to sell his motorcycle, no more hunting, no skiing, no hard bike riding, and no activity that could jar the neck. Ever.

We went out and bought Charlie the biggest truck I have ever seen. He wanted to make sure that if he got hit again, it wouldn't touch him.

This news killed Charlie. He started reflecting on why he'd lived from that accident. Then he realized why, again. It was because of the kids. I can vividly remember the day when he told me that he wasn't going hunting. Not knowing yet what the doctor had said, I was surprised. He then explained and said that his wife and children were more important. I was so proud of him.

"In 2015, suicide was the seventh leading cause of
death for males and
the 14th leading cause for females."
— Wikipedia, Suicide in the US 3/6/20

Let's lower these statistics.

DECEMBER 1998

Reckoning

The children continued to make progress, but it was clear that they weren't going to be home before the holidays. Charlie continued making strides with his business and was partnering with another man to create a new entity, servicing computers. I continued to go to the hospital.

By mid-month, Charlie was in another hospital to have his neck surgery. We could have waited, but two things rushed it. One: we were told that if he hit a bump in the road wrong, it could paralyze him for life if he didn't have the surgery. Two: the lawsuit had gone to mediation and the contingency of receiving the money was based on the surgery. Bastards. Well, no reason to waste any time.

Surgery was successful. I drove back in forth from each hospital to be with Charlie, then the kids. Charlie was supposed to rest and not move, but then again, this was Charlie. I think he wore the neck brace for 2 out of the 8 weeks before he was back working and making things happen.

He received a settlement for the accident that was enough to pay off all his debts, personal and professional, with a little to spare. He was debt free and happy!

Christmas was very low-key. We spent it with our children in the hospital. As most families wake up at Christmas to tear open gifts, we awoke to drive to the hospital to spend it with our precious and still very small children. It was divine. We had opened gifts from each other before the actual day of Christmas, as Charlie couldn't buy something for me and not give it to me just then. He loved to buy surprises, but just couldn't wait 'til Christmas to give them. We had a 16-foot tree that put that Christmas smell and spirit throughout the house. We could have been on a Christmas card; it was so picturesque.

We sent out a letter to our friends and family, telling them of our triumphs and pitfalls for the year and how 1999 would have to be better. Despite it all, we were happy, blessed, and in love.

On New Year's Eve, December 31, 1998, we were told that our little girl would be coming home in 2 days. We were so surprised. We couldn't think of a better present to end the year. We shopped for the house to prepare for her arrival, then went to our local watering hole to celebrate the New Year. We even told the nurses not to expect us, as we were going out to celebrate.

It was memorable. That I can say. We drank and reminisced until we got home, and it became evil. Nasty comments were made to each other. Charlie started to leave and said that was it; he wasn't coming back. I told him not to let the door hit him and to make sure he walked, as I'd paid for that new truck.

The next long moments were a blur, but I remember him going to the bedroom to get his revolver – a .357 magnum. I asked him what he thought he was doing, and he just yelled for me to go in the bedroom and forget about it. I was scared. For him and for me. I cried and cried and begged him to stop this. He paced and moved and carried the gun with him the whole time, loading and unloading it, screaming that he was going to get it over with. It was Russian roulette.

Two and a half hours later of begging, crying, and pleading, I convinced him to give me the gun.

It was after midnight, and I kept thinking that this was how we were starting the New Year. I went to bed and passed out.

I awoke in the morning too mentally and physically exhausted to care about anything. I sat in our bathroom, staring into the mirror. I felt like I was in there for an eternity. Charlie came in and stood behind me. He grabbed my shoulders, closed his eyes, and apologized. He promised it would never happen again.

I bowed my head.

I learned a long time ago to never say never.

"Firearms are one of the most common suicide methods globally. They are responsible for approximately 8% of global suicide deaths. But they play a much larger role in some countries. What stands out clearly is the very high firearm suicide rate in the United States—at over 6 deaths per 100,000 it's more than ten times greater than many countries across Europe. In the UK, for example, this rate is more than 30 times lower."
https://ourworldindata.org/suicide

Let's change these statistics.

JANUARY 1999

Arrivals

After 69 days in the hospital, on January 2, 1999, we brought our little girl home. Despite the recent events, it was the happiest day of our lives. We went to the NICU ward, took pictures, waved good-bye, tucked our 5-pound baby in, and nervously drove the one-mile home. We turned off all the phone ringers, put a sign on the front door, and looked at each other, wondering…what do we do next? The past two months seemed surreal, and this just added to it. Three days later, on January 5, 1999, we brought home our son with the same joy. Our circle was now complete. Our family was home together.

Whoever said that having twins couldn't be that more difficult obviously only had one child at a time. Somehow, it's more than double the work. There are three-hour intervals of feeding, changing, playing, and sleeping, only to do it again. And that's hoping they are on the same schedule. If not, then you are constantly feeding and changing, hoping to catch 5 minutes to yourself, even then, too tired to take advantage of it.

Although I have always considered myself good with children, it was usually with older children. I think it's because I talk to them like a friend versus a child, nephew, niece, etc. At the same time, I prefer to be with children than most adults. Who wouldn't? If I had an age to pick to live forever, it would be between 8-10 years old. No interest in the opposite sex, no real need for money, and your parents supply you with everything else you need. It's a glorious time.

Having two infants that weighed 10 pounds total was something I wasn't prepared for, even with them being in the hospital for so long. I have helped run companies with gross revenues of over 750 million dollars. I have been accountable for the largest revenue and expense categories of companies, and I can guarantee you right now that it is easier to do that than to raise a child (or, in our case, children). I have never been so mentally and physically exhausted. I take back all those times I thought my sister was a wuss for being a homemaker.

You know, they send you to child raising classes, but it doesn't help. You've probably helped your sister or brothers along the way with their children, but it's just not the same. It's like that movie *Parenthood* with Steve Martin and Keanu Reeves, which says something like, *"You have to have a license to fish, you have to have a license to drive, but any blankety-blank-blank can have a child."* It's so sad and so true. (And yes, I am a Keanu fan.)

The only true way you can learn to take care of a child is by experience. After two weeks, I thought I was going to fail.

Charlie was working nonstop, trying to build his business. He'd leave by 7am every morning. Charlie owned his own company. He'd never left before 9am before. I started to doubt he was working and thought he just wanted to get out of the house because it was so exhausting. By the time he came home, I was like a vegetable. He was scared I was going crazy. I didn't want to talk to my friends. Hell, I was too tired. The five minutes I did have, I didn't want to waste telling someone else how tired I was.

Charlie did everything he could to help me. He cooked dinner every night. Of course, he'd always cooked. He was an excellent cook and, more importantly, hated cleaning dishes. Whoever cooks, doesn't clean. He rubbed my back, feet, and shoulders. He even did laundry on occasion, after I lovingly showed him where the washer and dryer were located…again. After two weeks, we started taking shifts at night so we each could at least get 4 hours sleep. He had 10-2 and I had 2-6, but I also had every other shift after that, too, until he came home, which started being later and later. Not to mention, if the children woke up crying during his shift, I had to wake him to go get them.

How men can sleep through that amazes me. I now know why my mom had such keen hearing. Once you become a mother, it's programmed into you. At times, I feel I can hear a child crying from the neighbor's two doors down. It's scary.

By the end of the month, Charlie started scouting agencies to help us at home. Having no family living near that could help us, we needed someone just so I could sleep for a couple of hours or at least get out of the house. Charlie was seriously worried I was going to have a nervous breakdown. He was so used to me being in control that it upset him more than me. I just wanted a hot bath and 8 hours of continuous sleep.

No doubt, this was the hardest thing we had ever tackled, and it was getting hard to see the forest through the feedings. Although the joy of parenthood was still there, the responsibility of parenthood was TRYING.

The World Health Organization (WHO) and Institute of Health Metrics and Evaluation (IHME) often report data on self-harm, and use this term interchangeably with the term 'suicide'. This can be confusing, since self-harm and suicide are not generally considered to be synonyms. The term self-harm is often used by researchers to denote behavior that is not explicitly intended to lead to death. Some researchers go further and point out that self-harm and suicide attempts should be distinguished, because self-harm tends to involve more frequent but less severe injuries, so the distinction matters for identifying risk factors and providing help.
https://ourworldindata.org/suicide

Let's stop both!

FEBRUARY 1999

Steps

Meaning 12 Steps. Three days before Valentine's Day, we admitted Charlie into Charter Rehabilitation. The day started out so innocently for him….

A week into the month, Charlie didn't get out of bed for three days. I thought he was sick with the flu. I was actually getting into a routine with the kids, and I think I was so tired that I was learning to live on less than 4 hours of sleep. It was not till weeks later that I learned he was trying to decide where the best place to kill himself would be, and how. In the back yard? No, too much of a mess, and it would scare the dog. Upstairs? No, the kids are up there. Where, where, where? Shotgun? Pistol? Knife? Drugs?

Can you imagine? I couldn't, and still can't. It wouldn't be until three months later that I would understand that he knew exactly where and how he would finally do it.

A week later, my sister graciously offered to come to help with the kids for 5 days. Five days of heaven is how we saw it. After the second day, even she was worn out. She has three kids of her own. Charlie left for work, and we were going to have a big dinner that night. Curry Pork. He made excellent curry pork, with fried rice and sliced cucumbers with vinaigrette dressing. It was to die for. Charlie didn't make it home for dinner. We ate takeout.

Business and home life were getting to Charlie. That day, his largest account threatened to pull all their business. Charlie started drinking early. By 5'oclock when I called to ask where he was, you could hear him slurring. I prayed that this wouldn't happen while my sister was here. By 7pm, he said he'd be there in an hour. By 8pm, it was a different story.

Charlie came home at 11:00pm. He kept his promise…he made it home. He was unable to stand, and someone had dropped him off. I can only guess who. He snarled as he stumbled into the bedroom. I cringed as I tried not to watch my sister's reaction. I went back to talk to Charlie, knowing it was no use. He was in a fetal position in our closet. I left him there.

Twelve hours later, after not sleeping, myself, Charlie arose. He didn't know what to say but knew what I would say. I walked back into our bedroom and shut the door. He said he thought he needed help and wanted to go to Charter Rehab. He got dressed and headed to the door. I didn't stop him. I didn't say a word. I waited the thirty seconds until he returned to tell him that his brand-new truck was not here. He had no idea where it was and how he got home. I then drove him to Charter Rehab.

I was actually glad that it'd come to this point. At least he was getting help. I did, but also didn't, want to know where and who he was out with. Maybe now it would be different. He had so much going for him, but he was his worst nemesis.

Ever since we met, Charlie could never control his alcohol. Once he started, it was hard to stop. Not that we drank every day, but when we did, we generally blew it out. Over the years, I realized there was more to life. After I got pregnant, there was no choice…for me.

Charlie stayed in Charter for 4 days. It was a start. Due to his work, he justified why he still needed his phone, pager, etc. Most of the times the hospitals take these things away. They don't want you to talk to dealers, stragglers, bad influences, or whoever you call when you get sober or desperate. These places aren't the cheapest places, either. The irony is that the people that want to get help can't afford it, so they continue in their path of destruction, as they feel they have no other choice. Don't forget what I told you: Charlie is the smartest person I've ever met, so he was able to manipulate the system hands down.

We went through a thorough interview process describing his issues, past, and why he was there now. I told the counselors of the previous suicide attempts that I knew of. I knew there were more. I thought at the time that maybe it was due to alcoholism. Another hurdle that we would have to face. *Damn, when would we ever get a break?*

Each day, I visited him with the kids in tow. What a sight that must have been. If I was on the other side, I could only imagine what I would say or think. I figured that at least he was getting help, and that's more than most people can say. Although Charlie appreciated the program, he felt that he was above it. Most of the people there were hardcore. These are the types that put Jack Daniels in their windshield wiper fluid and rig it to squirt inside their car. We weren't at that point but had different issues all our own. Charlie couldn't grasp the 12-Step program and its religious tendencies. I couldn't blame him. It was hard for me to accept it, as he told me.

The hospital agreed that this may not be the best program for him but wanted him to continue on an outpatient basis. He had charmed them. Outpatient lasted for about a week, until another excuse came up as to why he couldn't attend.

While Charlie attended Charter, I started attending a weekly Al-Anon group. I really enjoyed it, too. Truthfully, I couldn't relate to most of the attendees, but I enjoyed sharing stories and hearing what others had been through. I'm not sure this group is for family/friends of alcoholics, but more about how to be a better person. We could all stand to attend.

In conjunction with this, we started marriage counseling, under my strong urging. We saw two counselors and we could both attest that they were completely incompetent. We wrote out goals for ourselves individually and for us as a family. My goals were typewritten and three pages long. Charlies were handwritten notes that fit on one page, but we shared many of the same values and beliefs about life.

Charlie has always been able to do whatever he wanted. Me, too. I believed that he could change to make this work. I've always known that the kids and I were the most important things in his life. He was just having a hard time adjusting. That's what I told myself. He felt that it was just a matter of more time, and that my pregnancy gave me a leg up, as I had to stop drinking. As these times progressed, I felt I was getting stronger and more independent. The counselors told us it was because I was a "survivor" and advocated for me to get out of this relationship. What did they know? This must have been frustrating and intimidating to Charlie, especially if you're codependent and the same advice was being repeated by everyone.

The countdown had started TICKING.

"Alcohol abuse is strongly linked to death by suicide.
In the US, in 2007 alcohol was involved in
approximately a third of reported suicides...
...Indeed, several academic studies have found a
positive and significant association between per capita
alcohol consumption and male suicide rates in a
number of countries."
https://ourworldindata.org/suicide

Know the signs.

The 12 steps to recovery.

1.   Honesty
2.   Faith
3.   Surrender
4.   Soul searching
5.   Integrity
6.   Acceptance
7.   Humility
8.   Willingness
9.   Forgiveness
10.   Maintenance
11.   Making Contact
12.   Service

MARCH 1999

Progression...in opposite directions

E ach week, we worked on our goals, attended different marriage counselors, talked late at night, discussed religion, work and beliefs, etc. I knew nothing had changed but hoped that we were at least starting in the right direction.

Looking back, I think that for Charlie, it was different. I think he had already made up his mind in February. It was just a matter of time. Like stalling an opponent in chess to make the final move.

We started working out and biking with the kids. Figured if both of us felt better physically, then mentally we would feel better, too. I wanted us to get in the habit of doing more family things, and this was a great way to get out. Charlie had some nice, expensive bikes and was an avid rider before his truck accident. I, on the other hand, am not an avid rider. My butt was sore for days. Athletic, yes, but toned butt (or, for that matter, any butt), no.

It was not even the end of the month before Charlie started drinking again. He may have been doing so the whole time prior—I don't know, it's all so unclear at times.

Charlie knew I had had it with him. If he couldn't even keep his promise not to drink for 30 days, how was this going to get any better? He knew I'd started thinking to myself that the children would be better off with one functioning parent rather than with two dysfunctional parents.

He called one night. Drunk, gun in mouth, he begged me to tell him why he shouldn't do it. This time, I would not have to take the gun from him but needed to convince him over the phone. I wasn't sure I had it in me. Like many of you, I still thought that this was a result of alcoholism versus something much deeper. I also felt that if you were that unhappy with your life, then just do it. Get it over with. If you can't see the big picture, then you might as well check out. *How naïve and stupid of me. How I wish I had known better.*

I told him to think about me and the kids and what that would do to us. I told him I loved him. He told me that he needed for me to say it all the time, so he would know. He had no self-value.

This time, luckily, he didn't succeed, but it was obvious that we both CHECKED OUT.

"While the link between suicide and mental disorders (in particular, depression and alcohol use disorders) is well established in high-income countries, many suicides happen impulsively in moments of crisis with a breakdown in the ability to deal with life stresses, such as financial problems, break-up or chronic pain and illness.

In addition, experiencing conflict, disaster, violence, abuse, or loss and a sense of isolation are strongly associated with suicidal behavior. Suicide rates are also high amongst vulnerable groups who experience discrimination, such as refugees and migrants; indigenous peoples; lesbian, gay, bisexual, transgender, intersex (LGBTI) persons; and prisoners. By far the strongest risk factor for suicide is a previous suicide attempt.
https://www.who.int/news-room/fact-sheets/detail/suicide

Be alert! Stay vigilant!

APRIL 1999

Fear

The drinking continued and continued. They always tell you that alcohol is a depressant, but Charlie took it to the next level…paranoia.

He felt that he could never overcome his latest actions, and how could he have any value in my eyes? So, he threatened divorce. Charlie never got over his first divorce. Not the fact that the marriage was over, but that she filed on him, not the other way around. Charlie was very religious, in some respects. Even though he had committed many of the cardinal sins, I don't think he would have ever filed for divorce, even though he wanted to. This time, though, his fear was coming out. He felt that he was going to lose me, so he'd better jump now. He probably wasn't going to lose me. I'd thoroughly believed he loved the kids and me more than anything and that he was going to make this work for all of us. It was just a matter of time. I could wait.

He took some things and moved out. The stalking began. I would see unknown cars check our mailbox. When and if he did come home, he was checking Caller ID. He disconnected my pager. He knew every one of my passwords and would check the computer when I was out of the house. He was waiting to catch me at something so he could justify the problem wasn't him, but me. He continued to drink.

One night, he returned in a fit of rage, saying that this would be the last time I'd see him. What was I to think? If he was willing to take his own life, what would stop him from taking mine—or worse yet, the children? I bolted with the kids to my sister's house. I had to get out of the house to feel safe again.

While I was gone, he appeared to sober up. He went to counselors. Called and apologized. Said he could make this work. Tricked me. He was stalling again.

One night while I was gone, Charlie scoured through the house and found old diaries of mine from high school. HIGH SCHOOL. He was vindicated. I had sinned, and he had proof. Proof that I was an idiot 15 years ago. I didn't even know I had the diaries. They had been in boxes I had moved over the years. They were memories long forgotten and didn't need to be restored.

He now wanted a DNA test again. Why? Because my past parallels yours? *Good God, get a grip.*

I returned home. I couldn't camp out forever and wanted to get on with my life. For another week, we attended more useless counseling. Each time, the counselors essentially told me to get out of the relationship. I remember thinking, "I thought you were here to help us. Do you hear us? HELP US!"

I remember crying, telling Charlie we needed help. We needed help.

Another binge, another phone call. This time, I changed the locks and kicked him out. I was scared. For the first time, I felt

I wasn't in control. In my heart, I knew that Charlie would never do anything to the kids or me—but this wasn't Charlie anymore. I decided I needed to take steps to protect us...physically, financially, and emotionally.

Another call. This time, we asked a mutual best friend to help us. Our friend basically came in as a mediator. Charlie agreed to stay at his house for 6 weeks. In that time, he had to come home every day to help with the children and show accountability. He had to leave after we put them to bed and, more importantly, no drinking. If he could manage to do this successfully, then, and only then could he move back into the house.

I had wanted 6 months. We agreed on 6 weeks. Charlie wouldn't live to see the OUTCOME.

"Suicidal ideation is one of the most common forms of crisis in therapy sessions that causes many clinicians great anxiety during and between sessions (McGlothlin, Rainey, and Kindsvatter, 2005). Therefore, it is important for clinicians to have a greater understanding of risk factors for suicide and knowledge on how to deal with concern for clients between sessions (Sharry, Darmody, and Madden, 2002). Risk factors for suicidal ideation or an attempt vary for each case. Researchers have identified that higher scores on the Beck Depression Inventory (BDI), higher frequency of domestic violence, previous attempts of suicide, substance abuse, poor economic situation, lack of close relationships, and a hopeless future orientation may be risk factors of suicidal ideation or a suicide attempt."
https://www.ncbi.nlm.nih.gov/pmc/

Be honest and give yourself forgiveness.

May 1-23ᴿᴰ, 1999

Completion

Before the end of the six weeks, I had a wedding to attend in Denver for a good friend. I had told Charlie that I didn't think it was a good idea for him to come, as these were all my friends (who knew what was happening) and, more importantly, I was tired. I wanted to get away, by myself. Charlie came with me.

The beginning of the trip was a wonderful experience. We were starting new. We went up a day early and went exploring and sightseeing. Charlie stopped on the highway, faking a flat tire, opened my car door, and proposed to me again. Charlie was a hopeless romantic. I couldn't even begin to count how many roses I received from him. It was all very…well, for a lack of a better description…picturesque.

Then I made a big mistake. I told him we could drink on the wedding day. I still wasn't convinced that Charlie had a drinking problem, but a mental problem that he was self-medicating. After that day, I realized that I was incorrect. Drinking was only a part, or a symptom, of a much bigger problem.

The ceremony and the view were spectacular. I was actually a "grooms women" in the wedding. As I stood up at the altar, Charlie was in the back-row mouthing "I love you." He had tears in his eyes. I'll never have to question if he really did love me. I knew that from the first day we met.

After the ceremony was over, I told him to meet up with us, as we had to take pictures. Charlie left with one of the groomsmen's date. She was a "looker," but a cheap looking one. Once pictures were completed, we all left for the reception. Charlie and the date weren't there, nor were they for another hour and a half. When they arrived, they were so smashed that they could barely stand. She commented to me that he talked all about me and how he loved me so much. I'm sure he did. I was pissed.

He couldn't understand why I was mad. Meanwhile, the girl was throwing up in the bathroom. How nice. I wasn't worried about what they could have been up to. I was disgusted that he was so drunk at this function. He passed out in the car and awoke one hour later, furious that I'd left him there. He then left me and headed for the airport. I knew he wasn't going to leave town. He didn't like traveling and it would have cost too much to change our tickets. He called at 11:30pm. I didn't answer. I later heard that he called his ex-wife and told her that he was going to commit suicide.

Surprisingly, we returned together the next morning, not speaking the entire flight. He asked what would be next. I told him that I finally realized that his problem wasn't just drinking, but he additionally had a serious depression or bi-polar problem that he needed help with. It was like a blinding flash of the obvious. I couldn't believe I'd never seen it before. How could I have missed this and been so unaware?

After the accident, the doctors told us that Charlie more than likely had a neuro misbalance. He was on Neurotin for the kindling of a focal brain injury and chemical and electrical sensitivity. Know what the pamphlet says? It says that stress may play a role in who becomes affected, but how big a role is still uncertain. It certainly increases the occurrence of "reactions," as does sleep deprivation, due to its effect on focal brain irritability. Charlie didn't sleep anymore.

For over 10 years that I have known Charlie, he had communicated that he wanted to commit suicide. I never thought much about it. I can't think about anything else, now. Maybe this truck accident had a greater impact mentally then what we knew? Am I reaching? I'll never know.

Charlie left the house and said that he was going to move into an apartment, as this was obviously going to take more than 6 weeks. I told him I thought it would be a good idea. I would only see him a few more times after he left.

In the remainder of this chapter, I will chronicle the events to the best of my knowledge…

Wednesday, May 19th, 2:00pm

I hadn't heard from Charlie since Sunday night. I didn't even try to call him. I didn't want to know what he was doing, or possibly with whom. He called mid-afternoon. This time, he was crying and had a shotgun in his mouth. I cried, too. This time, I realized that he needed so much help and that I couldn't be the one to help him. He begged me to tell him why he shouldn't do it, and that I loved him. It was always about me. He was obsessed with me. I begged him to go get help. Please, we need help, we need help!

Wednesday, May 19th, 5:00pm

Charlie called from Charter to tell me that he had re-checked himself in. Again, I was relieved and glad. Maybe this time it would work? He told me that they advised that he not talk to me on Thursday so he could fully concentrate on the program. He sounded good. He was glad he was doing this. He wanted to do this for the kids and me, but more importantly, for himself. I knew he could do it this time. I didn't feel anxious, angry, or anything. He told me that he loved me with everything he had. He called back 2 minutes later to tell me that when I called on Friday, he was admitted into the psych ward, as he told them he was suicidal. He would not be in the drug/alcohol abuse section. I felt him sigh.

Thursday, May 20th 3:00pm

Charlie came home. Charter Rehab had declined his coverage, saying that he was over his drug/alcohol abuse limit, based on my insurance coverage. I was enraged. First, he wasn't in for drugs and (2) he was in for psychiatric problems, and (3) more importantly, here was someone screaming for help. Goddamn, state commit him if you must. Charlie asked what he should do and then offered to pay cash until we could reconcile with insurance. If he had to sell his truck, guns, or whatever, he was going to do it. I was so proud of my husband. He returned to Charter and wrote a check.

Friday, May 21th

Someone from Charter asked to speak to me in regard to Charlie's "visit". I answered questions about why I thought he was there and how I felt. I told them about his multiple recent suicide attempts and how, at times, I felt that this was a copout, but realized that he had a major depression problem. Charlie later called to tell me how the day went and what they discussed and how this time he felt much better about it. He even gave them his pager and phone, as he was serious. At night, he called to wish me a good night and to tell me thanks and that he loved me.

Saturday, May 22st

I took the children up to see him. Just like the time before, he introduced and showed the kids and me off to the other "patrons." Charlie made friends everywhere. He made everyone feel so comfortable. He had an air about him that you just wanted to be near. We left, and I told him I would return to bring him some cigarettes.

Saturday, May 22st 6:00pm

I drove to Charter with the kids in the back and told him to meet me up front so I could drop the cigarettes off quickly. He was waiting for me like a schoolboy and told me how he'd just had a wonderful session and wanted to talk to me to tell me everything. I remember I started to drive off and he stopped me to give me a long, loving kiss. As I drove off, he mouthed "I love you." I smiled. I didn't realize that would be my last long kiss ever from my husband.

Saturday, May 22ˢᵗ 8:35pm:

Charlie was done for the evening and called to wish me good night, but more importantly, to tell me a joke he had just heard. It was completely inappropriate, and I laughed hysterically with him. We laughed until we cried. He then told me that he'd finally figured this out and, regardless, if he believed in this "higher power" that they preached, as long as he worked the 12 Steps, a miracle would happen. A miracle would happen. Those were his exact words. He believed it. I know he did.

Sunday, May 23ʳᵈ 6:00am

I awoke in a panic. The kids normally still woke up at least one time during the night. I thought that I was so tired that I may have slept right through it. Or worse yet, what if something was wrong? I ran upstairs to check on them and they were sound asleep. Ah, how nice. I went to the guest bedroom, as I was sure they would wake up soon.

Sunday, May 23ʳᵈ 6:35am

The phone rang. It was my dad. He had called yesterday, saying that my mom, who was a stroke survivor of 20 years, had been admitted to the hospital. He wasn't sure how bad it was but would call if there was anything wrong.

He told me to come home, as my mother would not make it through the day. I told him I would be on the next plane.

Sunday, May 23ʳᵈ 6:45am

I called Charter and told them I needed to speak to my husband and that it was a family emergency. Charlie got on the line and said, "Is it your mother?" I couldn't even talk. He said he would be home in a second.

Sunday, May 23rd 7:00am

I don't know how Charlie made it home so quickly. He came in the door, and I remember thinking how gorgeous he was. He hugged me and just kept saying how sorry he was and how much he loved me. I could barely speak. I told him that the kids were still asleep and that this was a bad sign. I kept thinking this was a bad sign. He told me not to worry about anything, just get going and he'd follow behind with the kids. I told him to wait until I got to San Antonio so I could assess the situation. I didn't want to uproot the kids if it wasn't necessary. He told me to just call him when I knew and hugged me again. This would be the last time I would see my husband or feel his strong, wonderful hug.

Sunday, May 23rd 8:30am

I was on the plane to San Antonio. What a sight I must have been. The pilot announced that there might be delays. I wept. The attendant gave me a Kleenex and I explained I was about to lose my mother. My mother!! I wrote down what I would have to say for her eulogy. I never got to give it.

Sunday, May 23rd 10:00am

My dad had waited on me to arrive before pulling the "plugs." When I saw my mother, she was already gone. I told him that she wouldn't want to continue this way. I said my final farewells to "Patty-Jo" my mom, my protector, my guardian. At 10:00am sharp, they turned off the machines.

Sunday, May 23rd 10:07am

At first it appeared that Mom might make a comeback, as her vital signs went up and down. The nurse explained to me that this just the body reacting to the machines. I watched until they read 0/0. It was 10:07am. My mother was dead.

Sunday, May 23 10:35am

I called Charlie. I cried as I told him how I'd just watched my mother die. He cried too and said how sorry he was that we didn't make it down for Mother's Day. I told him to hold off on coming until I could talk to my dad and see what kind of schedule we'd be on. I didn't want to have to make arrangements and take care of the kids, too. He said he would be waiting and that he loved me so much and was so sorry.

Sunday, May 23rd 12:35pm

We were already back at the house, planning and calling people. We were in denial. We were just processing. My sister and her husband had showed up 15 minutes after the machines were turned off. They were numb, too. I went outside and called Charlie and told him that I thought that he should wait until tomorrow to bring the kids, as there was too much I needed to do here. We talked about how we wanted to change our lives. I told him I wanted to move out of "pretentious Dallas." He was sitting in his office and told me that he was staring at a picture of him and me. He asked if I remembered the picture. Only too well. It was taken almost 8 years ago at an annual Christmas party I throw. I was in a red velvet dress in his arms and was looking back at the camera. Charlie told me that I looked so happy. I told him I was when I was with him. Again, he told me that he loved me so much. Me too, me too. The last thing he said was that if I wanted to drink, that it would be okay under the circumstances. In disgust, I said that would be the last thing I wanted to do. He quieted down and said, "I love you. Call me when you can."

Those were the last words and conversation we would ever have.

Sunday, May 23rd 2:35pm

I hadn't planned on calling Charlie, but I just needed to hear his voice. Instead, I heard a chaplain's voice telling me there had been an incident at the house. My first thought was the children. Oh my god, the children! He explained that the children were fine, it was with my husband. I was relieved, thinking it was only something minor. Then he told me my husband was dead. He had shot himself. As I was screaming in hysterics, our housekeeper and my sister were screaming also, trying to figure out what was wrong. I ran outside and said, "NO, NO, he can't be dead. He promised. Please tell me what happened? The children...please tell me about the children." I crumbled to my knees in the back yard. My brother-in-law came out and finished the conversation. He picked me up off the ground.

My husband was dead. He'd killed himself at 1:41pm, three hours and 34 minutes after my mother passed. I called back to make sure that a prayer was given at the house before the chaplain left.

Sunday, May 23rd 3:05pm

My dad returned from the funeral home. He had already been given the news and was trying to make it back to the house in time to tell me. He never even got to grieve for his wife of 43 years before he had to come home to get his youngest child and tell her that her husband was dead.

Sunday, May 23rd 4:05pm

I'm back on a flight to return home with my best friend. No one trusted leaving me alone. I had to get the kids. I arranged for my dear friend and their godmother to get them from the house. I'm calling anyone and everyone. I'm in shock.

Sunday, May23rd 6:05pm

I arrive to get the kids at my friend's house. It's decided that I would stay there until the house could be cleaned up. The house needed cleaning up…We try to figure what happened and to analyze everything. I'm so numb, I can't think. I know that Charlie must have left a note, an email, or a voicemail. I check everything. There is nothing.

Sunday, May 23rd 11:00pm

A priest who had been following Charlie's and my circumstances arrives to provide words of comfort. They were anything but that. Being brought up Catholic, and now being essentially an Easter and Christmas Catholic, I asked if Charlie was in hell for committing suicide. He replied that he didn't know, but it was clear that Charlie continually picked a path of destruction versus turning to God. He didn't have to say anything else. I knew what answer he was giving. I didn't believe it. I felt tormented.

The house is crowded, and everyone is asleep but me. I sit in the living room shaking my head.

I'll never know what exactly happened. From the scattered bits I did hear, this is what I do know…

Charlie had picked up a suit of his from his cousin to attend the funeral in San Antonio. His two brothers and their girlfriends and others are at the house. There is food and alcoholic beverages everywhere. Charlie is talking to everyone about our anniversary coming up and what we will be doing. He then looks at the kids and says, "I hope they know how much I love them." He excuses himself to the bathroom. With our children just outside the door, he shuts and locks our bedroom door and instantly fires a .357 magnum into the right side of his temple. His two brothers must break down the door to see their brother, best friend, mentor, and provider DEAD.

I have a lot of emotions that I still must resolve with this scenario. I don't understand how a patient who gets treatment and is released from a Center commits suicide just hours later. I don't understand why there is alcohol brought into our house knowing he was just released from a program. I don't understand how this happened four hours after my mother's death. I don't understand how he did it with the kids in the house. I don't understand a lot of things.

I know anger is a normal reaction. Don't get me wrong—I'm mad at myself too. I just didn't know and understand the magnitude of it all, or was it simply willed ignorance?

Charlie may have committed suicide at any time. It was his choice and his decision. I recognize that. He was also very sick. Looking back, each time that I think of alcoholism or depression, I wonder how I would have reacted if I'd inserted the words aneurysm or leukemia?

I never once looked up depression before Charlie did this. Ask me now. Do I feel guilty? How could I not?! Could I have made a difference? If I knew then what I do now, maybe, just maybe, he'd be here today. We will never know.

"WHO recognizes suicide as a public health priority. The first WHO World Suicide Report "Preventing suicide: a global imperative", published in 2014, aims to increase the awareness of the public health significance of suicide and suicide attempts and to make suicide prevention a high priority on the global public health agenda. It also aims to encourage and support countries to develop or strengthen comprehensive suicide prevention strategies in a multisectoral public health approach."
https://www.who.int/news-room/fact-sheets/detail/suicide

United we stand, divided we fall.
Stand together.

MAY 24-30TH, 1999

Mechanical

That's how you feel: like a robot. You just move. You don't think. That's how people cope, at first, when someone dies on good or bad terms.

As with my mother, I started making arrangements the next day. I was unable to see Charlie 'til the funeral home could "repair" his head. The bullet had entered his head, but never left it. I asked for a toxicology report to be done.

The support I received from friends, family, bosses, and co-workers was tremendous. Our mutual best friend, whom I had known from college and Charlie knew for over 10 years, was there by my side every second. My former COO and boss were at the funeral home to help me with any decisions and to lend support. People from out of everywhere and nowhere flocked to help. It added to the overwhelming sensations. At times, I just wanted to be alone. No one would allow that. They never said, but I'm sure they were worried about me and what I might do. I thought that was crazy.

Not having a religious affiliation in Dallas, I asked the chaplain that had found him to perform the services. He was a kind man and agreed and even arranged his schedule. Two days later, he would tell me that he couldn't add the verse that I had selected, as it referenced that God had closed Charlie's eyes and he is no longer in pain and is with him. He explained that Charlie closed his own eyes, and he didn't feel comfortable with saying this, as we don't know where Charlie is. I was outraged. I remember thinking, "We don't know where anyone is!!"

On Tuesday, I am able to see my husband. His eyes, of course, are closed and a little red. His cheeks are a little puffy. Otherwise, he looks really good. They did a real nice job with replacing hair over the bullet hole. I still don't believe it. Even now, as I type this, I still don't believe it.

I arrange for other family members and his ex-wife to view him privately. As awkward and painful as this was at times, it was the right thing to do.

That night, I fly back to San Antonio to meet with my family for my mother's viewing and service. Let me take a second to tell you about her...

I haven't mourned for my mother outside of my initial trip down to S.A. I don't know now if I ever will, under the circumstances. I'm sure I need to.

My mother had a stroke in 1978 that paralyzed her on her left side and left her mentally on a different level than before. She was witty and kind. She always smiled. Mom had a deep religious belief and strength. She raised five kids, and in my heart, I think she left this world on that day to help me.

When she first had her stroke and was in a bad condition, she always asked why she had lived. She'd wanted to die, also. I never considered this "suicidal" — she just didn't want to be a vegetable. This was easy to accept, for me. She was a vibrant woman before her stroke. Afterwards, she would have to rely on others (mainly my dad) for her day-to-day needs and relearn that she was still a vibrant woman.

She justified that she'd lived because she had unfinished business to attend to. Being the youngest of five kids, she lived long enough to see her baby married with two children. To me, she finished her business. Maybe she left because she needed to do one more thing for me? I hope so.

My second oldest brother gave the eulogy for my mom at her service and did a wonderful job. I feel sad, thinking that it should have been me up there.

Friends and co-workers of mine attended my mother's funeral, too. Amazing. I am blessed. I returned home to prepare for my own husband's viewing and service.

Throughout that week, I continually sing in my head the song *"Blue Skies, nothing but blue skies from now on...Oh, blue birds..."* Charlie and I had watched "Patch Adams" on our trip to Denver, and this was one of the songs in the movie. I think to myself that maybe this is his way of telling me he's OK.

We had watched another Robin Williams movie (can't recall the title), but the wife kills herself after the husband gets killed in an accident. I remember Charlie telling me that he, too, would rather be in Hell with me than in Heaven by himself. I told him that was not an option for me. I'd have our kids whom I'd have to raise.

Why do I think this has significance now? Because I know Charlie. Unlike most survivors of suicide that may never know why the other killed themselves, I think I do know why Charlie did this now. Piecing back the day's events, this is what I think went through his head at the instant he killed himself...

He's in the house with his brothers and others. He had asked them to take care of the house while we are gone, so they probably decided to make a fun day of it with pool, food, etc. Charlie talks to me and I tell him that he should wait 'til next day. He decides to have a drink with them. One becomes two.

Charlie is a deep thinker and had deep feelings. Very much more so than me. After he made the statement that it was okay to drink, he could tell I was disgusted, so he sat and thought about it. He had just been released from a drug and psychological rehab program, his wife's mother just died, he had the kids here, and he was drinking. Again. He was disgusted, too. Probably felt that he couldn't change. Looked around and thought I would be so disappointed right now over what was going on at the house. He couldn't live with that. He wanted the pain to be over. I feel like I know what he thought when he took his life. He thought the children and I would be better off. *Oh, Charlie.*

At first, I thought it might have been a combination of the medication and the alcohol as to why it was so instantaneous, this time. Before, he'd contemplated and agonized. The toxicology report proved me correct. He was legally drunk, though low, for Charlie's standards. He was legally considered drunk and now add in his prescriptive meds. Not a good combo.

On Thursday, I had the viewing for my husband. This would be the last time that anyone or I would see him, but he

81

would not be able to see us. I had already said goodbye to my husband, my friend, and the father of our children.

On Friday, I buried Charlie near a live-oak tree at Restland Funeral Home, the second largest cemetery in the United States. Beside him were spouses and loved ones born in the 1800's and laid here to rest. Charlie really was an old soul.

Probably 300 people attended the service. Family, friends and co-workers of mine, friends, and family of his, people he worked with, CEOs of companies, and even some Dallas Cowboy football players. Charlie made friends easily and he made them with those from all walks of life.

On Sunday, May 30th, I visited Charlie by myself and talked to him. You see, this was supposed to be a big day. Charlie would have turned 29 on this day.

He killed himself at 28 years of age.

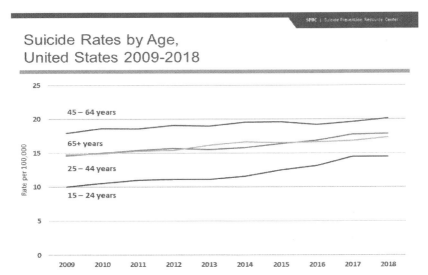

Suicide Rates by Age,
United States 2009-2018

http://www.sprc.org/scope/age

Let's change these statistics.

JUNE 1999

AnGrY. DENIAL. Fear. Shock. <u>Resentment</u>. Hardship. FRUStration. Relief? GUILT. Stigma!! ACCEPTANCE. Recovery. Life....

Did you know that there are 12 stages of grief? These aren't them, but they are close. I wonder if that is a coincidence with the other 12 Step programs? Maybe it's all a marketing ploy? Wouldn't that be a kicker?

Over and over, I have replayed every event in our life together. Many times, I didn't sleep, or couldn't sleep. I kept hoping and waiting for a sign. "Maybe it's the dog, or the wind chimes..." Not 'til moments later does it really sink in. He's never coming back.

Every day, I cried to myself. Some days, harder than others. I wonder if it ever will stop. Then I got scared. What if it does stop?

I haven't dreamed about Charlie, yet. I don't think I will be able to for a long time. I think about him roughly every second in my conscious moments. It's tiring.

What do you do next, after your loved one kills himself? In my situation, I had to move on, for our children's sake and for myself. Part of my self-healing is writing this. Time will be the other factor. I have a ways to go.

I can go on and on about the comments people have said to me after this. Inappropriate, in some cases. For example, "You're better off." My non-verbal reply was, *"Really? Great, then when your spouse dies, remind me to tell you that same thing. Jerk. Oh, I'm sorry, did I say that out loud?"* Or, here's another one of my favorites: *"You deserve better."* What the hell is wrong with people? I'm sure many meant and intended well, but unfortunately, it's not always communicated that way.

The people that will come out and support you will surprise you. Our neighborhood came out in full force, bringing the kids and I dinner and helping out with household chores. It was surprising and appreciated. It's amazing when strangers help. You feel awkward, but are relieved, and then realize that you must have touched their hearts and they, in return, touch yours by their generosity. Your situation also gives them perspective, and they are reminded that they are grateful for their life.

Many times, family and friends are the ones that are distant. They don't know what to say, so they often don't say anything at all. You feel isolated, then. At the end, each of us survivors will have to deal with this on our own. It's frightening.

I sent this letter out to reply to all the support I received:

June 13, 1999
Dear Family and Friends,

It's hard to believe it's been three weeks since the loss of both my husband and mother. I wish I had time to thank each of you personally for all the love and support you have given to my family and me during this quite difficult time. The support has been quite overwhelming. I am truly blessed to know and have each of you in my life. I want to thank everyone…be it for the prayers, flowers, food, coming from out of town, conversations, contributions, cards, tears, or hugs. Just knowing you were/are there has provided a sense of comfort to me.

I realize many of you have respected my space and didn't want to call until I'm ready. You never really know what to say to someone after a situation like this. In a matter of hours, in one single day, my whole world changed. I've gone through every emotion there is and have asked myself over a thousand times…why? I realize I can't ask why, as I'll never get a reply. So, I'll have to accept an old saying, "God grant me the serenity to accept what I cannot change, the courage to accept what I can, and the wisdom to know the difference."

I do feel a need to share with you a little about my mom and Charlie, so you can understand better what I may be feeling and not feel uncomfortable around the children or me. My mother was 65. She experienced a stroke over 20 years ago that paralyzed her completely on her left side. She had a zeal for life that is to be admired, but more importantly, she possessed an inner strength that we should all learn from. Although her death was unexpected, my family has had several near calls in the past that had somewhat prepared us. Not that you can ever be prepared when it happens. I know she is in a better place and is watching over all of us. Like a hawk!

My husband Charlie was a week short of 29. As most of you know, we had known each other for over 10 years, and the last year and a half has been filled with every possible scenario one could imagine, from truck accidents, marriage, and 70+ days in NICU with twins to neck surgery…the list could go on. His sudden and abrupt death has left others and I confused, sad, and/or angry. But what I have realized is that if you truly knew Charlie, you would know that he did not have control of himself when this happened. We should not be sad or angry but need to understand how this happens to someone. Suicide is the 9th largest killer in the US. White males commit three-fourths of suicides, with over 80% of caused by a major depression that is treatable if diagnosed accurately and in time. Most of us consider suicide as a sign of weakness when, in fact, it is a result of illness. At one point or another in our lifetime, one out of five of us will suffer from major depression. Look around at your friends and family. This could happen to someone you know. I pray that it doesn't. Charlie is also no longer in pain and is in a better place.

Charlie and I have two beautiful, healthy children that are now 7 and 1/2 months old. Wyatt looks like a little replica of Charlie and Taylar is a combination of my mother and myself. (Lord, help us all!) They keep me strong. They make me smile and they are my life.

One day, I will tell our children about all of this and how each of you has made an impact and a footstep in our lives. Our relationship(s) will not change, and we'll continue to share, cry, and laugh and will hopefully be better individuals from knowing and sharing with each other.

Thank you for being there for all of us and thank you for listening.

Michele, Wyatt and Taylar Jenkins

I attended grief counseling sessions shortly afterwards. There were mothers, fathers, spouses, and others in attendance. Each had a tragic story of their own. Their son had hung himself, one had one of their sons shoot himself right in front of them, and then their other son committed suicide 2 years afterwards. Others had their boyfriend die of carbon monoxide, and the list went on…

All were in different stages of coping. Some weren't able to cope at all. As I listened to them, I worried that some would never heal, and then I realized that maybe that was a step in my own healing. By the end of the sessions, I was probing and asking about their feelings and fears, telling them how I was dealing with it. And then I realized that maybe I could help them or others. After all, we learn by sharing. It gives us perspective and it gives us hope.

My life has moved on. It's different than what I had expected one year ago. Charlie and I would have been married one year in August. I went on our trip that we had planned to the Bahamas. It actually was a hellish trip. I hope Charlie was having a good laugh on me. He never wanted to vacation out of the US, and this trip was my idea.

Our children turned one in October. They are so precious. Our son really does look identical to Charlie. Identical. It makes me happy. Our daughter mirrors me. I have to laugh. If only Charlie could see them now. I hope he does. I think he does.

I had to start working again, for sanity's sake and for long-term financial security, and re-entered the cable industry while arranging to work out of the house. My children are my priority.

I still don't have all the answers, and maybe never will. I read anything and everything to help me understand. I read the Bible. I didn't before. It confuses me most of the time and makes me have more questions than answers. But, it's a start.

I'm not sure what is out there, but I do believe and feel this…We are not alone. Just look around. HE is there.

In the story of Genesis, the Testament says this…Take a recent "accident" you or a loved one may have suffered and acknowledge before God that it was no accident at all, but rather a stretching, maturing incident in his sovereign plan for you. I pray that this is true.

I'm still amazed at the simple things people take for granted…the telephone, indoor plumbing (big one), cable TV. How do you think these things get accomplished? Have you ever really thought what it takes to make a call to Singapore? We take it for granted, but it's really amazing. It's brilliant. It should serve as a daily reminder to say thank you.

Eighteen months. From beginning to end. The highs, the lows, the unexpected. Charlie and I shared 10 years and 18 months, but it's the latter that have changed my life forever.

A close friend reminded me of a song by Garth Brooks, *The Dance:*

…And I, I'm glad I didn't know, the way it all would end. The way it all would go. Our lives are better left to chance. I could have missed the pain. But I'd a had to miss the dance…

Someone asked me if I had any regrets. EVERY DAY, but I can't go back and change anything. But I can go forward and make choices. I choose to live with my children and be as happy as we possibly can be. I choose to cherish and remember the good memories Charlie and I had together. I choose to forgive my husband…and myself.

I often wonder, if Charlie were here today to see our children grow, if this would have made a difference. Another question I'll never know the answer to, but I just have hope and faith.

Although I relate to the Garth song, I often think of the following in my head:

18 months from beginning to end.
The highs, the lows, and ultimately the end.
The birth of our children,
The loss of my friend.

18 months is when it first started.
18 months then we were parted.

If I'd only known, but I guess that I couldn't.
Now looking at our children, I know that I wouldn't.
A life was taken, but three were given.
Three lives that have every reason for livin'.

There is no rhyme; there is no reason
There's only the changing of each season.

18 months from beginning to end.
How I miss you my love, my best friend.

There are many things I didn't share in this story. Great times that I will tell my children, other times that I will take with me. It is difficult for me to share this with friends and strangers. If you really read this, though, you'd understand, then, that this is not about me and this is not about Charlie…

**This is about people and life.
It's about an education.
This IS an unspoken pandemic.**

In 1999, suicide is now the 8th largest killer in the United States. Eight. One in every five people will suffer depression at some time during their life. We need to realize this is not a weakness, but an illness that is crippling to everyone involved. It's doesn't just affect the victim, but the survivors, as well.

I miss Charlie. I miss my husband and my friend. He adored and loved our children and me very much, and he made me laugh. Hard.

To my husband, I say…

"Fear not, as you are with us. Until we meet again.

I love you, Charlie."

We learn by sharing.
It gives us perspective and it gives us hope.

Spread hope.

THE YEAR 2023

I just celebrated my 22nd wedding anniversary with my second husband, Matt. We met at an industry work event roughly a year and a half after Charlie's passing. I was his client and was reluctant to do business with him. We married three months after we started dating. At the time, I vacillated, thinking I was crazy to get married so quickly, or was this destiny. I've been blessed.

Matt adopted the twins immediately after we married. We had another son in 2002 and moved from Plano to Southlake, Texas. We shared our story with only a few close friends at the time, or those that we felt could benefit from the information. We didn't share with others not because we were ashamed, but we wanted to spare and protect our young children from the harsh judgments and wrongful stigmas associated with suicide.

Our children knew the story and if/when they wanted to share with others, we left that choice to them. To our close friends and neighbors with whom we didn't share the story, we simply chose to be in the present. I didn't think I was lying. Just not sharing with others that possibly weren't invested in us. *I wish this was different.*

Our son, Wyatt, still looks identical to Charlie, and his sister, Taylar, mirrors me. Charlie's stepparents are in contact with our family and Wyatt went to meet Charlie's extended family for the first time. He loved every minute of it.

I'm sharing this story now, as the rates of suicide are alarming, in hopes that this can start a conversation about an unspoken killer that no one wants to talk about, but which surrounds each and every one of us.

In 1999, I didn't have 24-hour access to the internet and a plethora of information, but I still possessed a 'willed ignorance". Maybe it was naivety, vanity, exhaustion, or being self-absorbed—you name it—but I wish I could have done things differently and I made poor decisions in areas.

I should have started this conversation with more people a long time ago, but I can't dwell on that. Every day, our actions shape us, but I believe you choose what defines you.

I am a survivor of suicide.

It's time we all talked and started sharing information. Trust me, you don't want to have willed ignorance as your excuse. Not in this particular matter nor in any aspect of your life. This is my attempt at taking a willful stand. This is an unspoken pandemic that surrounds us.

In the United States alone at the time of this writing, due to Covid-19:

- thirty-six million people have filed for unemployment
- months/years of home schooling
- trillion-dollars new national debt
- alcohol and drug consumption on the rise

In the US, approximately 141 people have committed suicide in the amount of time you read this.

We must work together to change these statistics!

Please, I hope you can learn something from me.
We all need to stop with willful ignorance.
The next person to commit suicide may be someone you love.

I pray it isn't.

Ignorant {Ig-no-rance}
— The lack of knowledge or information. The word "ignorant" is an adjective that describes a person in the state of being unaware and can describe individuals who deliberately ignore or disregard important information or facts, or individuals who are unaware of important information or facts.

Willful ignorance (uncountable) (idiomatic, law)

— A decision in bad faith to avoid becoming informed about something so as to avoid having to make undesirable decisions that such information might prompt.

"Stigma, particularly surrounding mental disorders and suicide, means many people thinking of taking their own life or who have attempted suicide are not seeking help and are therefore not getting the help they need. The prevention of suicide has not been adequately addressed due to a lack of awareness of suicide as a major public health problem and the taboo in many societies to openly discuss it. To date, only a few countries have included suicide prevention among their health priorities and only 38 countries report having a national suicide prevention strategy. Raising community awareness and breaking down the taboo is important for countries to make progress in preventing suicide."
https://www.who.int/news-room/fact-sheets/detail/suicide

We NEED more awareness. We need ACTION.

KNOW THE SIGNS:

Major depression is characterized by five or more of the following symptoms being present during the same two-week period and representing a change from previous functioning.

- Depressed mood most of the day, nearly every day, as indicated by either subjective reports or as observed by others.
- Markedly diminished interest or pleasure in all, or almost all, activities for most of the day, or nearly every day.
- Significant weight loss when not dieting, or weight gain.
- Insomnia or hypersomnia nearly every day.
- Psychomotor agitation or retardation nearly every day.
- Fatigue or loss of energy nearly every day.
- Feelings of worthlessness or excessive or inappropriate guilt, which may be delusional, nearly every day.
- Diminished ability to think or concentrate, or indecisiveness, nearly every day.
- Recurrent thoughts of death, or suicidal ideation with or without a specific plan.
- Symptoms which cause significant distress or impairment in social, occupational, or other areas.
- The symptoms are not due to the direct physiological effects of substance or a general medical condition.

"There are several specific ways that social media can increase risk for pro-suicide behavior. Cyberbullying and cyber harassment, for example, are serious and prevalent problems. Cyberbullying typically refers to when a child or adolescent is intentionally and repeatedly targeted by another child or teen in the form of threats or harassments or is humiliated or embarrassed by means of cellular phones or Internet technologies such as e-mail, texting, social networking sites, or instant messaging. Cyber harassment and cyber stalking typically refer to these same actions when they involve adults. A review of data collected between 2004 and 2010 via survey studies indicate that lifetime cyberbullying victimization rates range from 20.8% to 40.6% and offending rates range from 11.5% to 20.1%."
https://www.ncbi.nlm.nih.gov/pmc/articles/PMC34779 10/

Again, we NEED more awareness. We need ACTION.

A special thank you to
Dan "Remmy" Stourac.
Incredible author, who provided insight and feedback in the
sharing of this story.

You'll want to read his incredible stories that will inspire you.

https://remmystourac.com

Michele Packard came from a military family and worked as a cable tv executive before staying at home to raise her three children. She has written in both the fiction and non-fiction genres, utilizing her experiences to share stories with others. She is a frequent traveler with her husband and is the primary caretaker of the family's beloved labs. Her fictional AESOP series is derived from real-life conspiracies and has won awards in the Fiction: Thriller categories from prestigious literary organizations.

Books by Packard
AESOP
FABLE
TELLER
COUNTERINTELLIGENCE
DEFCON

Scoochie-Scoochie Nite-Nite (Children's book)

Follow Michele:

Instagram:@aesopstories

Goodreads:@michelepackard

BookBub https://www.bookbub.com/profile/michele-packard

<u>www.michelepackard.com</u>

100% of net proceeds from this book will be entirely donated to national and local organizations, dedicated to supporting their endeavors in raising awareness for suicide prevention.

Made in the USA
Columbia, SC
17 October 2023